# Mark Twain

## An American Star

*written by* Elizabeth MacLeod

## Kids Can Press

# With much love to Blair Anderson and best wishes for lots of laughter in your life.

**Consultant:** Mark Woodhouse, Mark Twain Archivist, Elmira College

**Acknowledgments:** Many thanks to Mark Woodhouse for reviewing this book and making helpful comments and suggestions. I really appreciate his time and assistance.

As Mark Twain once said, "A successful book is not made of what is in it, but what is left out of it." I'm very grateful to my editor Chris McClymont for helping me with the tough decisions and improving the book so much. A big thank you also to editor Val Wyatt who began this series. Thanks as always to Karen Powers who has worked on this series from the beginning and has given such a terrific look to the books. I also really appreciate the efforts of Elizabeth Kelly, a great photo researcher.

Thanks for the interest and support of my dad and brothers, John and Douglas. And love always to Paul, my "Youth."

Kids Can Press acknowledges the financial support of the Government of Ontario, through the Ontario Media Development Corporation's Ontario Book Initiative; the Ontario Arts Council; the Canada Council for the Arts; and the Government of Canada, through the BPIDP, for our publishing activity.

Published in Canada by
Kids Can Press Ltd.
29 Birch Avenue
Toronto, ON  M4V 1E2

Published in the U.S. by
Kids Can Press Ltd.
2250 Military Road
Tonawanda, NY  14150

www.kidscanpress.com

Series editor: Valerie Wyatt
Edited by Christine McClymont
Designed by Karen Powers
Printed and bound in Singapore

The hardcover edition of this book is smyth sewn casebound.
The paperback edition of this book is limp sewn with a drawn-on cover.

CM 08 0 9 8 7 6 5 4 3 2 1
CM PA 08  0 9 8 7 6 5 4 3 2 1

**National Library of Canada Cataloguing in Publication Data**

MacLeod, Elizabeth
    Mark Twain : an American star / written by Elizabeth MacLeod.

(Snapshots: images of people and places in history)
Includes index.
ISBN 978-1-55337-908-9 (bound)
ISBN 978-1-55337-909-6 (pbk.)

1. Twain, Mark, 1835–1910—Juvenile literature. 2. Authors, American— 19th century—Biography—Juvenile literature. I. Title. II. Series.

PS1331.M25 2008     j818'.409

*Photo credits*

Every reasonable effort has been made to trace ownership of, and give accurate credit to, copyrighted material. Information that would enable the publisher to correct any discrepancies in future editions would be appreciated.

**Abbreviations**

t = top; b = bottom; c = center; l = left; r = right; MT = Mark Twain; HF = Huckleberry Finn; TS = Tom Sawyer

© **American Antiquarian Society:** 11 (newspaper); **California Historical Society:** 13 (br [TN-2350]); **Courtesy of the Cobalt Northern Ontario Mining Museum:** 13 (tl); **Courtesy of Elmira College, Elmira, New York/Home of the Center for Mark Twain Studies:** 17 (lt),19 (bl), 19 (bc), 29 (lb); © **Richard Embery Photography:** 19 (tl); **Courtesy of Dr. Rodger C. Evans, Biology Dept., Acadia University, Wolfville, Nova Scotia, Canada:** 21 (tl); **istockphoto.com:** 9 (tr [Andresr]), 27 (lc [Tony Campbell]); **Jupiterimages:** 29 (rb [Royalty-Free, Corbis]); **Library & Archives Canada:** 9 (lc [Line drawing of The Golden Press Works, Catalogue of Nineteenth Century Printing Presses/ Harold E. Sterne/AMICUS 479743/P. 245/nlc-946]); **Library of Congress, Geography and Map Div.:** 9 (b [G4164.H2A3 1869 .R8 Rug 127]); **Library of Congress, Prints & Photographs Div.:** 3 & 15 (MT, Instanbul [LC USZ62-2885]), 7 (bl [LC B8171-152-A]), 13 (tr [LC USZ6-105]) & (bl [LC USZ62-77569]), 15 (tr [LC USZ62-105992]), 22 ([LC-USZC2-2756]), 25 (postcard, kangaroo [cai 2a13773]) & (postcard, Taj Mahal [LC USZC-3582]); **Courtesy of the MacDonnell Mark Twain Collection, Austin, Texas/Photographed by Shea Waters:** 3 (bullfrog, TS cover, HF frontispiece); 7 (cr & bc & cr), 9 (rc [The Carpet Bag] & rb [house]), 10, 14, 17 (rb), 16 (all), 19 (tc), 18 (all), 23 (lt), 25 (rt & lt), 24, 19 (lb), 27 (lb), 29 (rc [translated eds.] & rt [Stormfield]); **The Mariner's Museum:** 11 (Pilot's cert. [P2175]); **Mark Twain Boyhood Home and Museum, Hannibal Missouri:** 11 (Henry); **The Mark Twain House & Museum, Hartford, Connecticut:** f. cover & 27 (MT in armchair), 1, 3 & 11 (steamboat), 4 (HF cover & MT signature), 5 (bc), 15 (b), 17 (house & Livy & MT), 19 (tr), 20, 21 (tc & tr), 23 (all except CT. Yankee illus.), 26; **Maxx Images:** 7 (t [GoodShoot]); **Glenn C. Meister Collection:** 11 (Keokuk [Courtesy of Jack Meister]); **Nevada Historical Society:** 9 (lt); **The New York Public Library:** 5 (tl [Print Collection, Miriam and Ira D. Wallach Division of Art, Prints and Photographs, The New York Public Library, Astor, Lenox and Tilden Foundations]); © **Darryl C. Rehr:** 19 (br); **Saranac Lake Free Library:** 27 (rb [Courtesy of the Adirondack Collection]); **Stock.xchng:** 5 (bl [© Dominic Morel]); **David Thomson:** 5 (tr [www.twainquotes.com/DaveThomson.html>]); **Toronto Reference Library (TRL) postcard collections:** 5, 7, 15, 25 ([postcard collections held by the TRL Picture Collection, and the TRL Special Collections, Baldwin Room]; **Courtesy of the Mark Twain Project, Bancroft Library, University of California, Berkeley:** 8 ([cased collection, 00001]), 12 ([1864.1]), 13 (bc [Scrapbook #4, 1864–1867]), 15 (Olivia [cased collection, 9.03c [02511]), 21 (bl [00108] & br [HF prelim. notes]), 25 (rb [16B/Tour Itinerary]); 27 (lt [Lyon 037]), 28 ([Lyon 054]), 29 (lt [00664]); **Special Collections, Vassar College Libraries:** 6, 11 (Sam portrait).

Kids Can Press is a *lorus*™ Entertainment company

# Contents

# Meet Mark Twain

*"Do the right thing. It will gratify some people and astonish the rest."*

— Mark Twain

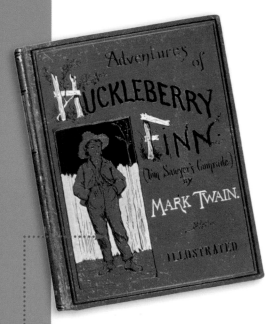

Mark's book *Adventures of Huckleberry Finn* changed literature around the world. Find out how on page 20.

Who could have dreamed that Sam Clemens, a poor boy from a tiny Mississippi town, would become one of the world's most famous writers? And more than just a writer—a comedian, world traveler and lecturer, too! Using the pen name Mark Twain, this southern boy grew up to become the first American celebrity.

Many people feel Mark was also the first truly American writer. "All modern American literature comes from one book by Mark Twain called *Huckleberry Finn*," said famous author Ernest Hemingway. "It's the best book we've had."

Not only were Mark's books considered the beginning of American literature, they also confronted the problems of racism and human rights in the United States. His most famous books, *The Adventures of Tom Sawyer* and *Adventures of Huckleberry Finn*, are still argued about. To this day, the books are both admired and banned.

Many readers love Mark for his humorous writing. But Mark often had little to laugh about. Misfortune seemed to walk in his family's footsteps. Mark's wife and three of his four children all died before him. He even went bankrupt. Despite these tragedies, he managed to keep his sense of humor.

Where did Mark get his ideas for his books? Why did he write the way he did? What was Mark really like?

*Why did I choose "Mark Twain" as my pen name? See pages 10 and 12.*

Hannibal, Mark's hometown, is located on the banks of the Mississippi River. The most exciting moment of every day was when a steamboat chugged into town.

BROOKLYN ACADEMY OF MUSIC, FEB. 7th

Tickets at 244 Fulton St. and 172 Montague St.

Here's a poster for one of Mark's speeches. People laughed out loud at the hilarious stories he told.

Mark grew up with lots of cats around the house. He loved cats all his life, especially kittens.

Mark traveled around the world, either gathering material for his books or giving lectures.

# Comet!

*"My mother had a great deal of trouble with me, but I think she enjoyed it."*
— Sam Clemens

Jane Lampton Clemens, Sam's mother, loved music, dancing and storytelling.

The night Samuel Langhorne Clemens was born, a comet blazed through the sky. Baby Sam was so sickly that his family called him "Little Sammy." Even his mother said, "I could see no promise in him." But she hoped the comet might be a sign of a bright future for her son. Sam would later say, "I was born excited."

Sam's family never had much money. His father, John Marshall Clemens, was a shopkeeper and a lawyer but had no luck in business. He moved his family around the southern United States often — they lived in five towns in about 12 years — always hoping he'd be successful. When Sam was born in 1835, the family was living in Florida, Missouri. Four years later, they moved to Hannibal, Missouri, on the Mississippi River. That move would be very important to Sam.

Hannibal was "a boy's paradise," according to Sam. He and his friends fished and swam in the river (Sam nearly drowned nine times!), explored nearby forests and caves and played pranks on people. Late at night, Sam would slip out of his bedroom window to find more adventure. School, he felt, was just something that got in the way of having fun. Sam loved to read and was a good speller, but he often played hooky.

Three times daily, big, beautiful steamboats stopped at Hannibal to take on or drop off supplies and passengers. These ships were driven by steam power that turned the propeller or a huge paddlewheel at the back. Sam and his friends admired the boats and idolized the men who piloted them.

Every summer, Sam headed to his uncle's farm back in Florida, Missouri. Sam loved cats — his mother did, too — so he always took one or two with him. At the farm, he played with his cousins and spent time with the Black slaves who worked for his uncle.

Sam had been taught that there was nothing wrong with slavery. In fact, his own family had a slave. But when he was young, he saw many examples of cruelty to enslaved people. In particular, Sam never forgot the sight of a group of African American men and women waiting in chains to be shipped to a slave market. "Those were the saddest faces I have ever seen," he remembered.

*I was born in Florida, Missouri, but my family moved to Hannibal when I was four.*

IOWA

ILLINOIS

KANSAS

Hannibal
Florida

MISSOURI

ARKANSAS

Mississippi River

The comet that streaked through the sky when Sam was born is called Halley's comet. It zooms by Earth every 76 years and will appear next in 2062.

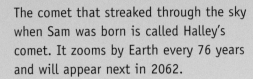

You can visit the museum that was built around the two-room shack in Florida, Missouri, where Sam was born. Find out more on page 32.

Sam loved talking and listening to the Black slaves on his uncle's farm. He never forgot the stories and songs they taught him.

Sam's childhood in Hannibal would later inspire him to create his best-known characters, Tom Sawyer and Huckleberry Finn. Tom was based on Sam himself.

# Southern boy

> *"Most parents think they know better than you do; and you can generally make more by humoring that superstition than you can by acting on your own better judgment."*
> — Sam Clemens

Sam was 15 when this photo was taken. He was working as an apprentice, or helper, to a printer.

By early 1847, when Sam was 11 years old, it seemed certain that his father would be elected assistant to the local judge and finally earn a steady income. But while he was out campaigning, Sam's father got soaked in a storm, developed pneumonia and died. Sam began walking in his sleep again, as he always did when upset. One night he terrified his mother and sister Pamela by sleepwalking — all tangled up in a white sheet.

To support her family, Sam's mother rented out rooms. His sister gave piano lessons, and his brother Orion (pronounced OR-ee-on), who was a printer in St. Louis, Missouri, sent home money. Sam could only attend school once in a while now — he was busy working as an errand boy, store clerk and blacksmith's assistant instead.

In 1848, Sam began working for the *Missouri Courier* newspaper. He earned no money but was promised a place to live, his meals and two new suits of clothes. His jobs ranged from lighting the fires that kept the offices warm to cleaning the printing press and folding and delivering the newspaper.

Instead of getting two new suits, Sam got just one — an old suit of his boss's that was far too big for Sam. Meals were skimpy, too. But Sam learned a lot. Part of his job was to read other newspapers and collect stories that the *Courier* could reprint. The young boy found out a lot about Hannibal and the rest of the world.

Sam still found time for adventure. One winter night, he and a friend skated far out on the frozen Mississippi. Suddenly the ice made a loud CRACK! Then it began breaking up. The boys raced for home, jumping from one sheet of ice to another.

Sam's older brother, Orion, returned to Hannibal in 1850 and opened his own newspaper, the *Hannibal Western Union*. Then he bought the *Hannibal Journal*. Sam worked for him, although Orion never had much money to pay him.

Sam discovered that he liked to write, especially funny stories. One time Orion left Sam in charge of the paper for a week. When he got home, Orion discovered that someone had showed up at the newspaper office with a shotgun because of Sam's stories — he didn't find them as funny as Sam did! Sam decided it was time to see more of the world.

When a hypnotist came to Hannibal, Sam pretended to let himself be hypnotized. Sam did so many outrageous things while seeming to be under a spell that he was the talk of the town for weeks.

Sam's first funny story was published in the *Carpet-Bag* in 1852.

Sam's brother Orion was ten years older than Sam and was his oldest sibling.

Sam helped print newspapers on machines like this one.

Hannibal gets its name from a famous army general who lived more than 2000 years ago. Because of the books Sam would later write, Hannibal has become known as "America's Hometown."

THE CARPET-BAG.
FOR THE AMUSEMENT OF THE READER.
VOL. II.
SPRING — A NEW VERSION.

*The house where I lived as a boy is now a museum* — see page 32.

# On the Mississippi

*"When I was a boy, there was but one permanent ambition among my comrades in our village on the west bank of the Mississippi River. That was, to be a steamboatman."*

— Sam Clemens

This illustration is from Sam's book, *Life on the Mississippi*. It shows Sam learning how to be a steamboat pilot.

After leaving Hannibal in the summer of 1853, Sam began working as a printer in St. Louis, Missouri. Then he headed east and worked in New York City and Philadelphia, Pennsylvania. But within a year, his brother Orion needed help with a print shop he had opened. Sam joined him in Muscatine, Iowa, and later in nearby Keokuk on the Mississippi River.

In February 1857, at the age of 21, Sam sailed down the Mississippi, determined to travel on to South America and make his fortune. But he changed his mind and began training to be a pilot on a Mississippi riverboat instead.

Sam had to learn all the landmarks and currents of the Mississippi River between New Orleans, Louisiana, and St. Louis — about 1930 km (1200 mi.) — and back again. He was also taught the special language the steamboat crew used. For instance, when the river was two fathoms deep — about 3.7 m (12 ft.) — it was called "mark twain." Pilots liked to hear this term because it meant the water was deep enough for their ships.

In 1858, Sam's younger brother, Henry, needed a job, so Sam got him work on a steamboat. Then Sam had a nightmare. In his dream, he saw Henry lying dead in a metal coffin, wearing one of Sam's suits and holding roses. Sam's mother had always thought he had the ability to see the future, but Sam hoped this dream wouldn't come true.

Just a few months later, there was a fire on Henry's steamboat. He was badly burned and died within a week. Henry was buried just as Sam had dreamed. The young pilot was devastated and blamed himself for his brother's death.

Sam still loved piloting the big ships and thought he'd do it for the rest of his life. But the American Civil War broke out in 1861. This was a battle between the Union States, which were mostly in the north, and the Confederate States of America, which were the southern states. The main reason for the war was that the southerners wanted to continue using African American slaves, while northerners felt this was wrong.

Soon it was no longer safe for riverboats to steam along the Mississippi. Sam couldn't be a pilot and he didn't want to fight on either side in the Civil War. What would he do now?

As a pilot, I earned $250 a month — as much as America's vice president. And I was only 22!

This pilot certificate was issued to Sam in St. Louis on April 9, 1859.

When Sam (left) and his brother Henry (below) were growing up, Henry was always well-behaved — unlike mischievous Sam.

*City of Memphis* was one of the steamboats that Sam helped pilot.

Many newspapers carried articles about the steamship explosion that killed Henry.

Sam, his brother Orion and their mother all lived in Keokuk around 1855. The first articles Sam ever wrote and was paid for were printed in Orion's shop here.

EXPLOSION OF THE Steamer Pennsylvania.

Dispatch to the Associated Press.

MEMPHIS, June 14.

The Railroad Steam Packet Pennsylvania exploded her boiler Sunday morning at six o'clock, at Ship Island, seventy miles below Memphis, and burned to the water's edge.

There were about 350 passengers on board, and it is believed that a hundred of them are killed and missing. The steamers Diana, Imperial and Frisbie picked up all they could find in the water and took them ashore.

The following is a list of the lost, saved, the following is at present known:

# A new name

*"It ain't what you don't know that gets you into trouble. It's what you know for sure that just ain't so."*
— Mark Twain

Back in Hannibal, Sam decided to join 14 friends to fight for the southern states. But none of the young men liked the idea of battle, and the unit broke up after two weeks.

Then Sam's brother Orion offered him work again. Orion had just been given the important job of secretary of the new Territory of Nevada (it wouldn't become a state until 1864). But Orion couldn't pay for his ticket there. So he offered to make Sam his assistant — if Sam would pay both their fares. Sam agreed and, in July 1861, the brothers headed west.

Sam was amazed by the vast deserts of Utah and Nevada. Some days it was so hot that Sam, wearing only his underwear, sat on top of the stagecoach. From up there he could get a good look at the scenery. Three weeks later, the brothers pulled into Carson City, Nevada's capital.

It was soon clear to Sam that his job involved no duties and no pay. So he and a friend explored nearby Lake Tahoe. They marked off an area of forest that they planned to buy and dreamed of becoming rich by selling the lumber. But Sam was careless with a campfire, and the trees — and the two pals' dreams — literally went up in smoke.

Next, Sam tried mining for silver, like so many others who had come to the territory. And, like most silver seekers, he had no luck. Then in 1862, he became a newspaper reporter for the *Virginia City Territorial Enterprise* in Nevada. Sam loved this work. When he couldn't find real news to write about, he invented it. He also chose a new name for himself, inspired by his steamboat days: Mark Twain (see page 10).

It wasn't long before Mark wanted to be on the move again. He worked for the *San Francisco Morning Call* newspaper in California, but when he began writing articles that annoyed lots of people, his boss let him go. By the end of 1864, Mark had no work and no money. He was so depressed that he actually considered suicide.

In January 1865, a friend convinced Mark to visit the mining camps in Calaveras County in the foothills of California's Sierra Mountains. There Mark heard a funny story about a gambler who would bet on anything — even a jumping frog. That story would change Mark's life.

Mark was already known for giving humorous speeches when this picture was taken in 1864.

Sam rode across the United States in a stagecoach like this one. The coaches stopped about every 16 km (10 mi.) to replace the tired horses with fresh ones so the vehicles could keep moving swiftly.

The discovery of silver in western Nevada in 1859 was one of the biggest mineral finds in the world. Over the next year, 17 000 prospectors poured into the area, hoping to strike it rich.

*My pen name, "Mark Twain," first appeared in print on February 3, 1863, in the* Territorial Enterprise *newspaper.*

OFFICE OF THE
TERRITORIAL ENTERPRISE

EARTH QUAKEY TIMES,
SAN FRANCISCO, OCT. 6, 1865.

Sam was in San Francisco in 1865 when a violent earthquake hit. He wrote, "... the ground seemed to roll under me in waves."

# The jumping frog

*"The difference between the right word and the almost right word is the difference between lightning and the lightning bug."*
— Mark Twain

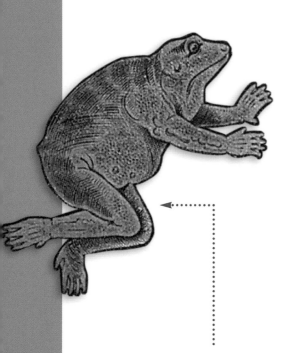

This is the jumping frog from Mark's hilarious story. A stranger got the better of the gambler by feeding the frog lead pellets until it was too heavy to leap!

Mark wrote down the story he'd heard at the mining camp about the gambler and the frog. He told it so well that it was soon published in newspapers across the United States. Readers loved the tale. A top magazine called it "the finest piece of humorous literature yet produced in America."

By the time Mark's story, "The Celebrated Jumping Frog of Calaveras County," was published in 1865, the Civil War was finally over. Enslavement of African Americans was now illegal, but racist groups of White Americans sprang up to terrorize and kill former slaves. Mark was disgusted and angered by these activities.

In March 1866, the *Sacramento Union* newspaper sent Mark to Hawaii for four months to write about the islands. The articles he sent back were funny, informative and very popular. But when Mark returned to California, he was desperate for cash again. A friend suggested that Mark give talks about Hawaii. He nervously agreed.

Mark didn't need to worry. People who had read his articles now wanted to see him in person. They attended his talks ready to laugh, but they were also impressed with his vivid descriptions. Mark knew how to perform his stories well, and his audience loved him. Mark loved the $400 he earned for just one night's work. He continued lecturing and became America's first star.

In early 1867, Mark moved to New York City. He gathered together some of his best stories and, on May 1, his first book was published: *The Celebrated Jumping Frog of Calaveras County.* About a month later, he began a five-month cruise to the Mediterranean and wrote a series of articles about the trip.

During the tour, Mark became friends with a young man named Charles Langdon. When Charles showed Mark a photo of his sister, Olivia, Mark immediately fell in love and begged Charles to introduce her to him. Soon after the cruise ended, Mark finally met the lovely, delicate young woman. He knew at once that, more than anything else, he wanted to marry Olivia.

Mark had to go on a lecture tour across the United States to earn money. But he wrote to Olivia frequently, and by November 1868 they were engaged.

*I had fun writing this notice for my first lecture. The people who came expected a good laugh, and I didn't disappoint them.*

This photo of Mark was taken when he visited Turkey during his Mediterranean trip.

When Mark saw a photo of Olivia Langdon, he immediately fell in love with her. "[Olivia] is the most perfect gem of womankind that ever I saw in my life," he said.

During his tour of Europe, Mark visited many countries, including Egypt (above), France, Italy and Turkey.

Mark saw dancers like these when he visited the Hawaiian islands. At the time, Hawaii was called the Sandwich Islands.

Mark cruised to the Mediterranean aboard this ship, the *Quaker City*. It was the first luxury cruise ship ever to set sail from America.

**Amusements.**

**_IRE'S ACADEMY OF MUSIC**
**The Sandwich Islands!**
**MARK TWAIN,**
(Honolulu Correspondent of the Sacramento Union)
will deliver a
**Lecture on the Sandwich Islands,**
AT THE ACADEMY
ON TUESDAY EVENIN

In which passing mention w
Bishop Staley, the American
the absurd Customs and Ch
tives duly discussed and
VOLCANO OF KILAUEA
attention.

A SPLENDID ORCHESTRA
Is in town, but has not been engaged.
ALSO,
A DEN OF FEROCIOUS WILD BEASTS
Will be on Exhibition in the next Block.
MAGNIFICENT FIREWORKS
Were in contemplation for this occasion, but the
idea has been abandoned.
A GRAND TORCHLIGHT PROCESSION
May be expected; in fact, the public are privileged
to expect whatever they please.

Dress Circle..............$1 | Family Circle......50 cts.
Doors open at 7 o'clock.  The Trouble to be-
gin at 8 o'clock.                          se28-td
Box Office open Monday, at 9 o'clock, when seats
may be secured without extra charge.

# Yankee in Connecticut

*"Wrinkles should merely indicate where smiles have been."*
— Mark Twain

Mark invented a self-adjusting clothing strap, a history game and, in 1872, a self-pasting scrapbook with pre-printed strips of glue on the pages.

*The scrapbook was the only one of my inventions that earned me any money.*

In 1869, Mark published *The Innocents Abroad,* a book based on his Mediterranean trip. It was an instant bestseller and one of Mark's most popular books ever. Mark was promoted as "The People's Author," since readers didn't need to be highly educated to enjoy his writing.

On February 2, 1870, Mark married Olivia, whom he called Livy — she called him Youth. Mark was then part owner of the *Buffalo Express* newspaper, so the couple moved to Buffalo, New York. Their house was bought and furnished by Livy's father. Livy asked Mark to tell her stories about his boyhood, and the questions she asked would later inspire Mark to write some of his best books.

Livy and Mark's first child, Langdon, was born prematurely in November 1870. The little boy caught colds easily and was never healthy. Adding to the family's problems, Livy developed typhoid fever, a very dangerous disease, and nearly died.

Soon after Livy recovered, Mark sold their house and his portion of the Buffalo newspaper and moved the family to Hartford, Connecticut. At that time, it was considered the richest and most beautiful city in the United States. Mark needed to make money for his family, so he went back to giving public lectures around the country. He also tried inventing and created three new products.

Mark returned home in early 1872, just as his book *Roughing It* was published. This latest work was loosely based on Mark's time in Nevada and California. In March, his daughter Olivia Susan (her family called her Susy) was born. Sadly, his son, Langdon, died in June. A few weeks later, Mark had to sail to England for a lecture tour. There, he was called the most popular American writer ever.

In December 1873, *The Gilded Age* hit the stores. This book was co-written by Mark and his friend Charles Dudley Warner and was about corruption in the United States in the mid-1800s. Soon Mark and Livy had another daughter, Clara Langdon, who was born in June 1874.

Three months later, the young family moved into a house that was built just for them. Most people considered it strange-looking — someone said it looked like a steamboat — but the family loved their new home. It was so huge that they needed seven servants to run it. The house was lavishly decorated, especially when Mark and Livy prepared extravagant Christmas celebrations for their daughters.

Langdon Clemens was only 19 months old when he died. Mark blamed himself for letting his son catch cold during a carriage ride.

One Hartford newspaper called Mark's house "one of the oddest looking buildings in the State ever designed for a dwelling, if not in the whole country."

Mark loved wearing unique outfits. Few people had a sealskin coat like this one.

Livy began proofreading and editing Mark's manuscripts. She would help Mark in this way for the rest of her life.

Susy was three years old and Clara was one when this photo was taken.

| 1896–1900 | Mark and family live in various cities in Europe |
| 1900–1903 | Mark and family return to the United States and live in New York |
| 1903 | Mark and family travel to Florence, Italy, for Livy's health |
| 1904 | June 5 — Livy dies in Florence |
| 1905 | Mark lives in New York |
| 1906 | Mark organizes the Aquarium Club for young girls he calls "Angelfish" |
| 1907 | Mark receives an honorary degree from Oxford University |
| 1908 | June 18 — Mark moves into his last home, Stormfield, in Redding, Connecticut |
| 1909 | December 24 — Jean dies at Stormfield |
| 1910 | April 21 — Mark dies of heart problems at Stormfield |

## Mark's books

How many of Mark's books and stories have you read?

| Published | Title |
| --- | --- |
| 1867 | The Celebrated Jumping Frog of Calaveras County |
| 1869 | The Innocents Abroad |
| 1872 | Roughing It |
| 1873 | The Gilded Age |
| 1873 | Choice Humorous Works of Mark Twain |
| 1875 | Sketches New and Old |
| 1876 | The Adventures of Tom Sawyer |
| 1880 | A Tramp Abroad |
| 1881 | The Prince and the Pauper |
| 1883 | Life on the Mississippi |
| 1885 | Adventures of Huckleberry Finn |
| 1889 | A Connecticut Yankee in King Arthur's Court |
| 1892 | The American Claimant |
| 1893 | The £1,000,000 Bank Note |
| 1894 | Tom Sawyer Abroad |
| | The Tragedy of Pudd'nhead Wilson |
| 1896 | Personal Recollections of Joan of Arc |
| | Tom Sawyer, Detective |
| 1897 | How to Tell a Story |
| | Following the Equator |
| 1900 | The Man That Corrupted Hadleyburg |
| 1902 | A Double-Barrelled Detective Story |
| 1903 | My Début as a Literary Person |
| 1904 | Extracts from Adam's Diary |
| 1906 | The $30,000 Bequest |
| | Eve's Diary |
| | What Is Man? |
| 1907 | A Horse's Tale |
| 1909 | Is Shakespeare Dead? |
| | Extract from Captain Stormfield's Visit to Heaven |
| 1916 | The Mysterious Stranger |
| 1924 | Mark Twain's Autobiography |
| 1935 | Mark Twain's Notebook |
| 1962 | Letters from the Earth |

*"The best way to cheer yourself up is to try to cheer somebody else up."*

# Visit Mark

### Mark Twain Birthplace State Historic Site
Florida, Missouri

Located on the Mark Twain Lake Reservoir, this site includes a museum built around the small house where Mark was born.

### Mark Twain Boyhood Home and Museum
Hannibal, Missouri

You can visit the home where the Clemens family lived from 1844 to 1853. Close by is the home of the girl who was the model for Becky Thatcher in *Tom Sawyer*.

### The Mark Twain House and Museum
Hartford, Connecticut

This museum is in the house where Mark lived from 1874 to 1891. Here he wrote *Tom Sawyer*, *Huckleberry Finn* and *A Connecticut Yankee*

### The Mark Twain Study
Elmira College in Elmira, New York

At Elmira College, you'll find the building where Mark wrote *Tom Sawyer* and many other books. It was moved here from nearby Quarry Farm. Mark and Livy are buried nearby.

*See the places that inspired my stories!*

# Index